The Tongues
We Speak

Books by Patricia Goedicke

Between Oceans, Harcourt Brace & World, 1968

For The Four Corners, Ithaca House, 1976

The Trail That Turns On Itself, Ithaca House, 1978

The Dog That Was Barking Yesterday, Lynx House Press, 1980

Crossing The Same River, University of Massachusetts Press, 1980

The King Of Childhood, Confluence Press, 1984

The Wind Of Our Going, Copper Canyon Press, 1985

Listen, Love, Barnwood Press, 1986

New and Selected Poems

The Tongues We Speak

Patricia Goedicke

MILKWEED EDITIONS

THE TONGUES WE SPEAK

Printed in the United States of America.
Published in 1989 by MILKWEED EDITIONS.
Post Office Box 3226
Minneapolis, Minnesota 55403

Books may be ordered from the above address.

92 91 90   4 3 2

Milkweed Editions gratefully acknowledges the funding support of the Jerome Foundation, the First Bank Systems Foundation, the Dayton Hudson Foundation for Dayton's and Target Stores, United Arts (through the Arts Development Fund), the Literature Program of the National Endowment for the Arts, and the generosity of individual donors.

LIBRARY OF CONGRESS CATALOGING-IN-PUBLICATION DATA

Goedicke, Patricia.
  The tongues we speak : new and selected poems
by Patricia Goedicke.
      p.   cm.
  ISBN 0-915943-34-3 : $9.95
  I. Title.
PS3557.032T66   1989
811.54–dc 19
                                        89-3105
                                        CIP

ACKNOWLEDGEMENTS

The author gratefully acknowledges the following journals for the publication of poems not included in her previous books of poetry:

The Gettysburg Review, Volume 1, No. 2, Spring 1988: "Lost in Translation," "Mountainside Farm"; *The Graham House Review*, No. 11, 1988: "Dear Presence"; *The Massachusetts Review*, Winter 1988: "After Lovemaking"; *The New York Quarterly*, No. 34, Fall 1987: "Who Goes There"; *Northern Lights*, March/April 1987: "The Hills in Half Light."

For Leonard, As Always

The Tongues We Speak

VIII NEW POEMS

I

IN MY FATHER'S TOWER

Proudflesh

A thousand Edens lost, and autumn
In the garden of old men
Is fall, is aimless, is a parade of pain,
Is Adam old in vain:
Who whispers I have sinned
Cries the dry flag limp upon the wind.

Age snickers in its sty
Or blesses, afraid to cry
Summers too soon gone by.
My father counts his disappearing past,
My mother mutters all her days
A faded ritual of praise.
Joseph and Mary and infant me
Slip between her fingers
One, two, three,
But out in the garden the trees
Trumpet their scarlet lecheries.

Lascivious as lips, the leaves
Fall on my father where he grieves:
Though he will not look he sees
Me, standing at his knees.

He turns away, he licks his lips and spits,
My mother sullenly repeats my name,
And fingering their fears they sit
Secret, ashamed, whose penitence is vain:

Eden begins again,
and out in the garden I
Parade triumphant by.

In My Father's Tower

Pickled brains in the cellar!
True:
My father the doctor kept them,

Real ones, human
Quivering like sponges,

Old cantaloupe rinds
Floating in a tan crock.

Sneaking my ten year old looks at them
I thought they were someone's lost soul,

I thought brains were everything.

All night, terrified,
I laid my head down in them like an old bathing cap,
I wore them like water wings when I studied math.

The King my father had pickled them and hid them:
I knew how important they were.

Wearing scholastic letters they stalked my dreams,
But billing them as all powerful

As bat droppings, magic fingers,
Dangerous skunk cabbage

I showed them off to my friends,
I swore by them and earned everyone's praise

And then languished for twelve years
In my father's tower
Living on dead brains

Until you came, my athlete,
My dear with a dumb kiss

And now farewell to the cellar:

Cabbage head's a flower
Wetter than any mouth,
Dearer than mind to me

And richer, ranker, growing

Like a golden egg from my forehead,
Like a live red soul from my shoulders.

In The Ocean

At first my mother would be shy
Leaving my lame father behind

But then she would tuck up her bathing cap
And fly into the water like a dolphin,

Slippery as bamboo she would bend
Everywhere, everywhere I remember

For though he would often be criticizing her,
Blaming her, finding fault

Behind her back he would talk about her
All through our childhood, to me and my sister,

She rarely spoke against him

Except to take us by the hand
In the ocean we would laugh together

As we never did, on dry land

Because he was an invalid
Usually she was silent

But this once, on her deathbed

Hearing me tell it she remembered
Almost before I did, and she smiled

One more time to think of it,
How, with the waves crashing at our feet,

Slithering all over her wet skin

[18]

We would rub against her like minnows
We would flow between her legs, in the surf

Smooth as spaghetti she would hold us
Close against her like small polliwogs climbing

All over her as if she were a hill,
A hill that moved, our element

But hers also, safe
In the oval of each other's arms

This once she would be weightless
As guiltless, utterly free

Of all but what she loved
Smoothly, with no hard edges,

My long beautiful mother
In her white bathing cap, crowned

Like an enormous lily

Over the brown arrow of her body,
The limber poles of her legs,

The strong cheekbones, and the shadows
Like fluid lavender, everywhere

In a rainbow of breaking foam

Looping and sliding through the waves
We would swim together as one

Mother and sea calves gliding,
Floating as if all three of us were flying.

The Cure

(For Helen Mulvey McKenna)

1900–1969

1

Before they knew it,
what had been happening
for years,

the claw of cancer hooked
that gentle Irish
tough pebble of a woman,

born in Boston, "brought up"
by a herd of red-headed
platitude spouting bully-boys.

Deaf since childhood, tossed
from one set of loud heroes
to the next,

having hung helpless for so long
in the bleak smokehouses of her sorrow
finally she cured herself:

a glacial empress, tiny
in her emerald gown,

muttering silently on the icy flanks
and mountainsides of her suffering

she turned into a great Chinese lady
and went off climbing alone.

2

And would not let them come near.

Having brought them all up
to the level of her courage, first

the stiff gray husband, that dour
lame frozen lighthouse,
then the withdrawn, sour
secretly writing daughter,

by main force having wooed them
a little way into warmth,

at last, on the royal throne
of the final kingdom of silence

under the crown of her pain she shut
and locked the palace gates.

3
In the cave of herself curled up
like a small stubborn animal

in the middle of the vast, glittering
formal antechamber she must have sat

waiting?

God knows what
doing or thinking she would not say

when they had to leave her for the night
never asked them to stay.

4
As soon drag honey
from stone

sound of bees from silence

for all the gardens they ignored
and she cultivated for years.

Eagerly, flushed with tenderness,
having invited them to the party,
the golf course, the sunset,
the passionately simple
dramatic discussions of art, politics
over and over and been refused

in death it was her turn.

Too much on her mind to bother
one could say:

certainly she would say
in the glib irony that helped keep
all but the most persistent pilgrims away.

5
Speak to me, tell me
I kept begging

over and over wheedling
like a commoner for life at her skirts

this / now / your
suffering's too much

for the fire I left that is empty
for the teakettle turned to stone

forgive us, please
the climate of loneliness is cold

but No, she answered, No. . . .

6
And still foolishly I kept saying

Spirit of zinnias,
spirit of leaves, labyrinths

Though none may accompany another,
hid in the conch of your ear

is the secret machinery of the verses
your speechlessness spun
from my desperate tongue

not for myself, but forever
for love, for touching
for you to remember, to recite

to lull yourself to sleep
over and over and over
the long hospital nights.

7
But slowly I began to learn
there is no breathing so endless
as that which will not stop.

And when there is failure of speech, finally
whether of poetry or love
the cure for it is silence . . .

Yet once, / yet

the eyes like wildflowers opened
on the brush of the back of a wind

the fragile hand raised itself
to my cheek and stayed

lifted on a smile that sank
lightly onto the air, wordless

but infinitesimally powerful
"as a petal floating on the Grand Canyon"
she used to quote to me

the impact a poem makes
or a life.

II

CROSSING THE SAME RIVER

That Was the Fruit of My Orchard

No moon. No night
    Either.
        White as the inside of an onion

Bed after hospital bed stretches
    Endlessly to the sky.

In the shadowless country of loss
    Wafers of silence whirr,
        Knives like hummingbirds flicker.

Silently they insert the needles,
    The scalpel cuts across
        The entire melon gapes open

And they scoop it out with a spoon
    Silently they throw it
        Where?

I, who was not there, tell you
    That was no nightmare.

Now, even though the scar lies
    Hidden under the grass

Sodium pentothal still blooms
    Coldly, everything smells of ether
        And everything keeps murmuring

Loss is an endless column, cry
    Without sound, mute
        Bird that has flown too high,

And that was the fruit of my orchard
    They plucked

That was the field of my body
    They trampled

I, who was not there, tell you
    That was no nightmare.

In the Waiting Room

Carrying my illness to the hospital
Everyday, carefully
As if it were a rare gift

I think I am something special,
I want everyone to pity me, to exclaim,

But lost in the hubbub on the main floor
There is so much merriment I could cry.

Among all the expensive flower arrangements
Like small hedges to conceal the truth

Upstairs there is gossip, there is nervous laughter
But downstairs it is quiet,
Outside the radiotherapy room

The patients stick together, in the half-light
Awkwardly leaning themselves against the wall

Like barnacles on a dim raft,
Defenseless as marshmallows, hunched,
Stuffed into their gray hospital sacks

And shivering a little, in the cold
Feeling their frayed bandages

They nod but they do not speak,
The thin man with the moustache,
The woman in dark glasses

Sitting on the edge of pain
They absolutely refuse to share my grief

And suddenly it occurs to me,
In all honesty they are only interested in their own,
There is nothing special about it,

Settling uneasily among them
I stop poking at myself, oddly
But finally relieved, at home.

In the Hospital

When they came at me with sharp knives
I put perfume under my nose,

When they knocked me out on the operating table
I dreamed I was flying

When they asked me embarrassing questions
I remembered the clouds in the sky,

When they were about to drown me
I floated

On their inquisitive glances I drifted
Like a leaf becalmed in a pool.

When they laid harsh hands on me
I thought of fireworks I had seen with you,

When they told me I was sick and might die
I left them and went away with you to where I live,

When they took off my right breast
I gave it to them.

My Mother's /My / Death /Birthday

Now almost everything I ever imagined
Has caught up with me:
The death-defying leap that worked,
The desert years that flowered,
Now the shadow has found a bed to lie down in,
I have come back from the cemetery of divorce:
Having sucked strength
From her tears, turned
Her denial into second growth
Now in my 39th year as if it were the 9th month
Heavy with summer, filled
to overflowing by the good man
She always meant me to marry,
I see him standing like an orchard
Over all the dry days of her dying:
Though the ache of her absence is the first bruise
On the blossoming plum she bore
Now even as the world descends
My mother my mold my maker
Is with me to the end:
Now the hand in the glove of the body,
The soul moves freely and well,
Pockets rolling with the stars of the one man
I always meant to love and now can.

Hands That Have Waved Farewell

Hands that have waved farewell
Meaning, we will meet again,

Cities I had thought lost forever
That have returned to me,

Sooner or later I will see them again, the mountains
The white coffee cup beside my plate

Steaming in the cold, as suddenly solid
As the most miraculous happening

In the whole world, it is a gift
That is given to everyone, yes

Everyone:
The patterns of our lives

Repeat themselves, like the old woman
Who keeps looking into your eyes from a window

Right next to the tracks as the train passes
On its way to forgotten farmhouses,

The strict pine trees of New Hampshire
Like night watchmen in the snow...

For me it was a small town in Mexico
Flamboyant, full of flowers

Lying on a hillside with the moon
And bittersweet stars in its hair

But for me also it was the one man
I did not recognize,

At every turning point in my life
Like a small pony he would be standing there

Like an armchair with a cello in it, or a brook
He kept beckoning to me like the sun

Or a coffee cup, full of warmth
Until I accepted him, so that now

In the thick snows of New Hampshire,
In the dry deserts of Mexico

Over and over I keep finding them
Rustling in the wind like leaves,

Like growth rings in the book of trees
Hands that have waved farewell,

Cities I had thought lost forever
That have returned to me.

All the Princes of Heaven

First it is only the sense of sunlight
Creeping up over the dunes

Darkness is beginning to pale
Imperceptible sounds

In every corner of the house there are shiftings
Minute, barely distinguishable

The delicate slow tide rises
Out on the long marshes

Something is running through the tall grass
Crinkling it with excitement

Inside, it is as if they were moving furniture
The heavy velvet of the couch
Blunders over to the window

The crisp curtains are beginning to breathe
Fronds of your hair sweep
Back and forth along the floor

Out on the porch of your thighs
Sandpipers flicker, with their little feet

From one fiber to the next
The flat wooden planks are beginning to swell

Now the seagulls are impatient, mewing
And flapping their wide wings,

Turning your quiet abdomen into a loud
Fourth of July day crowd

With flags waving, people
Jostling each other in the street

Your breasts are beginning to ache,
They are turning into Scylla and Charybdis

But softer, with hearts of butter,
Nipples of pure cream

Your teeth open and close like the jaws
Of a ravenous whale but gentle,
Rolling in its own sweet wake

The inner and outer lips are turning purple
Stretching themselves like a child sucking

The agitated motion of the round pilings
On either side of the dock increases

Waves slap back and forth
Both buttocks are jerking

The white galaxies of night
Inhabit the day, in a trance

The orange prow of the ship appears
Over the horizon it shoves its way
Across the smooth sheets

Shooting stars and colored streamers
And twenty-one gun salutes

All the princes of heaven come
Leaping onto the land,

Exploding together into dawn
The earth shakes itself to pieces,

In the hot arms of the sun
The sides of the waiting wharf heave
Up to the sky and then down.

The Arrival

Luggage first, the lining of his suit jacket dangling
As always, just when you'd given up hope
Nimbly he backs out of the taxi

Eyes nervously extending, like brave crabs
Everywhere at once, keeping track of his papers
He pilots himself into the home berth

Like a small tug in a cloud of seagulls
Worries flutter around him so thick
It takes him some time to arrive

And you wonder if he's ever really been happy:
When the blue eyes blur
And stare out to sea

Whether it's only a daydream
Or a long pain that silences him
In such gray distances

You'll never know, but now
Turning to you, the delicate mouth
Like a magician

Is curious, sensitive, playing tricks,
Pouting like a wise turtle
It seems he has a secret

With the driver,
With the stewardess on the airplane
So that even when he opens his arms

When the warm voice surrounds you,
Wraps you in rough bliss,
Just before you go under

Suddenly you remember:
The beloved does not come
From nowhere: out of himself, alone

Often he comes slowly, carefully
After a long taxi ride
Past many beautiful men and women

And many dead bodies,
Mysterious and important companions.

Daily the Ocean Between Us
(Psalm for my 43rd)

After the first shallows have dropped away
Leaving us gasping for breath

Suddenly the air is much thicker.
I swim in it, almost choking
Except for you

It is as if we had fallen into a blood pudding.

Wave upon wave of it rises,
Slowly the hot heaviness settles. . .

After 43 years I'm still struggling to get through
These sodden labyrinths that have sprung up

Everywhere around us:
Roots, water snakes, lilies. . .

Surely it is a kind of pleasure, this pain.

In the tender suck of the bayou
Mangroves caress our knees

But also there is this slow,
Powerful, deep pull:

In between rages, red-faced
Here we are holding hands

Under water there is this current
Flowing like lava between us:

[40]

Teaching each other how to breathe
Gradually we move out to the center:
Wrestling together in the dark

At least, for awhile, we keep going,
We fight side by side,

Each of us embraces the other
With fists or kisses, no matter:

Whenever you shift, I shift
From one stroke to the other,

Daily the ocean between us
Grows deeper but not wider.

Crossing the Same River

For the Continuity Man splices
Scene / after scene
Together

And then throws them away / helpless
Because they keep changing

They refuse to stay the same

They will gather no moss
He insists

Nobody ever took photographs of us
As children

We have changed,
Changed entirely from the time

In the quick burst
Of a flashbulb

Someone once said
Hold still / darling
Hold still. . ..

But I will remember
And you will remember

What we said before:

No bigger than a moth's shadow
With soft shaky wings

Something in us
Persists:

From one decade
To the next / registering

However delicately / pictures
That become part of us

What each of us is
And will be

Layers of living
Accumulate

Breath after breath / no heavier
Than marsh lights

Though the skin seems
To slough off

Flakes of mica
Disappear

For every imprint
There is a negative

For every forgotten flower

Quietly closeted / somewhere
For every hand there is another

In the cloudy folds
Of the brain

Everything we have ever known

Is only waiting for its opposite
Its other half to leap

Into the positive light

Clapped in its bronze arms
And swinging

Back and forth like bells
Endlessly touching each other / out loud

The almost invisible / the one
Smallest fraction grows

Into the giant watermelon of the tongue
Banging back and forth / and spurting

Foaming / fizzing / cascading
The brilliant amber of its voice beating

Into the open marigold of a body

That stays in one place / leaving
Only to return again

In such gallant continuity
The high ancient paean
Of the bell towers of mankind

The huge metal sails vibrate
Like a hive of singing bees

The liquid notes peal
Every hour on the hour

The sweet, steadfast cells of love
Forever replacing each other / and ringing

III

THE OUTER BANKS

In the Twilight Zone All I Know Is the Commercials

Big things in the wind:
Big dirty things in the wind.

All across America is that OUR underwear
Flapping on the clotheslines are those OUR mangy sheets

WELL I'D LIKE TO KNOW WHOSE THEY ARE

Gleaming like Abraham Lincoln's spectacles
Are those my false teeth

Is that Thomas Jefferson's flying heartache
Do those moth-eaten buffalo belong to me

WELL I'D LIKE TO KNOW WHOSE THEY ARE

Rolling around above me like a baseball
Is that my Babe Ruth, is that MY President
Eavesdropping on the other team's plays,

Is that my scandal with the sincere hair and the baby blue eyes,
Is that my True Confessions, my tape recorder, my home-made bomb,

WELL I'D LIKE TO KNOW WHOSE THEY ARE

If I'm committing the sin of pride please stop me,
I MEAN I'M A RESPONSIBLE CITIZEN

Every four years I vote but I can't help it,
Who can predict what will happen
In the Twilight Zone all I know is the commercials,

But if those aren't my Congressmen or my Senators
If those aren't my brown babies

If those aren't my Jews
Expelled again, from the new Eden

Getting into the same old cattlecars, and wailing
like tattered black birds across the heavens

WELL I'D LIKE TO KNOW WHOSE THEY ARE

Happiness

At first it fills you entirely,
Enveloped in it there's no room anywhere
For any other feeling,

It seems almost you could rise
Infinitely expandable, like hot air

Forever floating in a balloon,

The kind seen ascending
Over football stadiums and slaughterhouses,

Red, green, gold
The colors of victory

Chrysanthemums like shaggy dogs
Barking for joy in the wind

Your cheeks hurt from smiling
but the one next to you kisses them

Or tumbles, head over toes
Ridiculous as a flopeared puppy

The spirit of a grown man or a woman
Clowning its way into the heavens

Inside you feel like water
Resting in a clear lagoon

Everything is so peaceful here
Not an ache anywhere

There's nothing to do but listen
Up in the blue sky watching

The tall white cumulus clouds,
Calm chords of the cathedral
Of the sunlit aisles of happiness

All you have to do is sail away

Except that it's so *boring* here, all alone
You keep telling yourself it can't last

But this is what it means
To lose yourself, resistless

In every corner, in a world
Made of pure air

Forget it all,
Forget everyone and everything

And you can't do it, you can't let go, at the end

Down in the football stadium there you are,
That small dark blotch in the crowd holding on
To the wrong end of the string.

At the Center of Everything Which Is Dying

You swear you are as healthy as the next person,
Like anyone else you despise pain,
At every election you are innocent of war

But inside you there's a swamp
That keeps pulling you towards it.

Waiting for the next outbreak of the disease,
The next rifle shot, the explosion

Almost as if you had a secret lover
Faceless, waiting for you in a closet

You keep looking for it everywhere,
At board meetings, at every planning session

Sucking the possibility of catastrophe
As if it were a sore tooth

At the center of everything, which is dying
The ooze of pus attracts you,
Soldiers and chronic invalids

Have nothing to do but obey orders,
All the difficulties of life are done for them

As on a sickbed one forgets everything,
Centering on the self only

Even when the surface of the onion is pure
Gradually the soft spot, the delicious rot

Keeps seeping outwards
From one layer to the next

Inside everyone it is possible there's a viciousness,
A lascivious finger beckoning

Pornographic as sex
Without love there's a stink
Inside everyone it is possible

There's a stagnant pool that wants to be fed
New bodies, every day.

Mea Culpa

For whether it is the President of the United States
Or just some ordinary citizen at the piano

Drunk, at midnight, in the middle of Watergate weeping
Over the old songs,

The establishment is always likely to be your father.

It is a gift they have, for burrowing beneath your ribs
Like large babies with guns looking for sanctuary.

Beware the divided man who has been given too much power!

We know what happened to Lear, whom we invented,
To proud Lucifer fallen
And now Jehovah:

Beware the divided man who has been without women too long.

No wonder he has to play the piano to himself at midnight:
He thinks the other half of being strong is being strong.

Whenever his wife and his two daughters try to talk to him

He refuses to listen, he goes downstairs to pour out his heart
To the gold strings of the piano.

How tenderly he strokes, he caresses his own image!

He crouches over the keyboard like a boy
Kneeling before his mother's lap.

He thinks of himself as a cripple and he is:
Someone pitied him when he was young and he never recovered.

Will Rachmaninoff, will Jerome Kern talk back to him?
No, they will only tranquilize him with sweet sadness.

Closed in on himself like a clam
He wrings such misery from the music
You want to resist him but who can?

In public he is so powerful, so sophisticated! Natty
As a Doberman Pinscher in his neat cuffs

He tells us he is only a poor fork
Looking for its mate

But living with him is like living in the ten stomachs of a snake.

Whimpering to himself, at home
In scuffed slippers he limps
Piteously, through all our dreams.

Next morning we come down to find chunks of waste meat
And spent ammunition clips littered all over the cave.

Yet the man sweats, sneezes,
Sobs like any of the rest of us.

Can he help it
If we appointed him to play God?

Beware the divided man who wants only to be loved.

Clasping the entire cross to himself
He insists it is all his fault:

He knows his own hungers

But can't stop:
He says he has a trick knee

But swaying back and forth like Tchaikovsky
Or Brahms, heavily rising and falling

In a movie about lost love
And a lone tree high above the Pacific

How would he know that standing on one foot at a time
Is the way everyone walks?

At Every Major Airport

Dear Passengers, I hate to sound reactionary about this,
But even if you believe you really *are* in His hands,
Even if you are able to pray like my husband
(Who also takes sleeping tablets, and drinks)

There's no getting around it, unfortunately
I think you had better be ready to die
When you fly.

The sheer terror of it has been written about often
In poetry, in prose—
Even therapy groups have been formed to combat this fear

But it can't be helped,
Always
At every major airport in the world

First you have to crawl through a caterpillar
Lugging your hand luggage up its guts,
Next through an open gate, a scream
Exhaust tearing at your hair

And then you're in for it:
Thumb closes the door
And you, poor miniature you
Whether you smile nervously at the stewardess
Or cling to the soft pad of the palm

By God you better know it:
That old belly of an earth mother just rolled over,
Stuck up a couple of hands
And caught you, just like that.

Right back in the old coffin, uterus, icebox
There you go again:

Driving an automobile it's easy to get out
Whenever you want to, even a bus or a train stops
Once in awhile, at country crossings

But not here, thousands of miles high,
Nobody stops here,
Even He doesn't stop here
Or, if He does
His intentions are by no means absolutely clear—

Better just lean forward and use the vomit bag
And remember you have nothing to fear but the man

Who, after all, invented this whole business but which one?
The one with the pistol that looks like a Didee doll,
The kind that can pee blood all over the whole cabin,

Or the man who, after inventing this next-to-impossible machine
Of course finds it hard to believe in a God about Whom
However, there have been several well documented reports:

How, over Lake Pontchartrain, in Louisiana, the pilot said he felt
"As if a huge Hand suddenly grabbed the ship and tossed it up in the air
And then let go"

Whereupon the pilot regained control but there are other incidents,
Squawks over the recording device,

"It's as if . . . . someone's . . . . got hold of us . . ."
Then silence,
Then the scream of the wind
Picked up after the crash.

Escalator

Meeting me it was love at first sight:
You named me for my aspirations.

Ascending with me like a serpent's tongue
Into the one heaven of a department store

You called me water flowing uphill
As smooth, as calm

One foot sliding into
The other and that one
Into the next and so

On like a caterpillar unfolding
On bird's feet, precise
Liquid

Jeweled belt going up
Yes truly I am a dream machine
Riding me no one speaks

Electric
Noise bubbles and boils

Like the tubes of a Moog Synthesizer
Yards and yards of me coil
From the basement to the mezzanine

Expanding, contracting, in paradise
Like a zipper silently opening

Up again, down again, smooth
In slow motion hunted

As you, lordly, rise
Without moving hand or foot
Past everything you ever wanted.

You Could Pick It Up

You could pick it up by the loose flap of a roof
and all the houses would come up together
in the same pattern attached, inseparable

white cubes, olive trees, flowers
dangling from your hand
a few donkey hooves might stick out

flailing the air for balance,
but the old women would cling like sea urchins
and no children would fall.

Even though it is small,
the people are Greek, and it sits
like an oyster in the middle of the Aegean

still it is tough, it reminds you
of wagon trains, prairie schooners
drawn up in circles by night

you could swing it around your head
and still nothing would happen,
it would stay

solid, the white walls
rising up out of the sea
the pillared crown of the temple...

For twenty-six hundred years
it has endured everything, but now
we who have forgotten everything,

we whose homes have all gone
to super highways, belt cities, long thin lines
our glittering buses snort into the main square,

the spider web with sticky fingers
glues itself to the town,
slowly it begins to revolve, faster and faster

tighter and tighter it is wound
till the young men cannot stand it,
they pack up and leave town

the sky is full of children
with wild eyes and huge faces
falling to the ground.

Gloria Dávila From Texas

Many times I have seen innocence asleep
Beside me in the calm bedroom,

In the smoothness of white buttocks, the two pads
Of a water lily spread out on the sheets.

How fresh it is, how exciting,
On the verge of a new country, on vacation

With sprays of flame colored bougainvillea,
With corn roasting, cactus blossoms, the bright sparks

Of coffee beans drifting across the mesa,

The tender embroidery of the breath
Weaves in and out, my eyes open

On such sweetness, the morning filled with air,

Outside our windows the whole of Latin America
Stretches itself to its full length,

With oceans on either side, bays, lighthouses, cliffs,
The narrow beaches of conquerors,

And suddenly I'm nauseated,
Boiling in hot sweat, angry

Thinking about hunger with its cracked feet,
Its blood pouring from the body

Where most of us can't see it, at the waist
In Central America the fountains

Spurt from the steps of the cathedrals
In waterfalls of young students, torn shirts,

Bullet holes and mouths gaping

Everywhere, even in this classroom
Here where I stand, behind the lectern raving

That it's all useless, everyone's too old,
Too selfish to do anything. . .

But then Gloria speaks to me, Gloria Dávila from Texas

In worn blue jeans, with her light voice
Quiet and earnest as an ant.

She'd much rather go back to the white bread,
To the ice cream of the United States,

But over the ancient land bridge,
Underneath everything she hears them,

The small feet of her ancestors shuffling
Like water trickling, thousands of tiny streams

Nourishing an entire continent,

And she won't let herself go back,
At least not for awhile,

She wants to do translations, she is young,
In the bare libraries abstract as a nun

She pulls dictionaries around her,
In the toothpick boat of her pencil she sets forth

On the rough surfaces of the song
Of all the poets of Latin America,

That great mocha-colored river like a crocodile
Invisible as molasses, the slow jaws twining

Around our hips with the flashing
Of silver scales, the crushing weight of snakes

Shouting from the treetops like the brass trumpets,
The tattered bands of the poor...

For the rags of such language are a banner
Full of parrots and wild flames,

The hands of history beckon
From every bedroom,

The sigh of oppression is a wreath of buzzards
Knowing their time will come, revolving

In slow, voluptuous circles turning
Implacable as an alarm clock going off

In the white heart of everyone,
Even innocence, waking

To the red steel mills and the green orchids
Of Latin America, of work and Gloria waiting.

The Outer Banks
(June 6, 1968)

With most of the good men gone, the great
Society itself crumbling,
Out of Ohio through the Blue Mountains
On the day of his death I drove down
To the thin edge of the sea.

The shoreline is different this year.
New gouges, ugly inlets, more
Ground given away

As always,
Even in Ohio, everywhere
The roots of the land are dark diggers.

But what is the speech of seagulls?

The rhetoric of love is hunger.
Snap, like a shot
The fingers grab, the assassin's shovel
Swallows whole hillsides in the night—

We are the eaters of earth, eaters
Of the substance, ourselves,
The flesh sliding away to the sea
The trees torn up like teeth

By a seagull's naked beak plunged
Into the rhetoric of death
That is the final hunger.

Back up on the beach.

An old woman like a peasant
Bent, in black, shuffles along
Looking for shells? At her age?

Yugoslavia among the rubble. After the war
Only the crones remain,

But even as the gulls rise
With a great lifting of tattered skirts
Hacking and spitting they cry

The rhetoric of love is also hunger
To pick up the pieces, observe
The woman has a brand-new permanent,
There's a gleam
In the beady eye of every old bird.

It is as good, good enough
As any place to be.

My green bubble of a car pops
And snorts in the shifting sand.
Back of me this huge, proud,
Dark looming land.

We do not understand what
Holds us together;
Like children we keep on and on
Looking for something to blame.

In the forests the fingers of the trees
Knead, twist, hold hands

But the fault's built in, underground
Oceans suck at our weak knees,
The dunes erode, like weathered heads
Grow balder everyday—

What is the speech of seagulls?
The rhetoric of love is hunger.
I want more, the rich

Want more, and the poor—
But here, at the edge of the sea, what
Holds us together is less.

We must build more on less.

IV

THE TONGUES WE SPEAK

The Tongues We Speak

I have arrived here after taking many steps
Over the kitchen floors of friends and through their lives.

The dun-colored hills have been good to me
And the gold rivers.

I have loved chrysanthemums, and children:
I have been grandmother to some.

In one pocket I have hidden chocolates from you
And knives.

Speaking my real thoughts to no one

In bars and at lecterns I have told the truth
Fairly often, but hardly ever to myself.

I have not cried out against the crimes of my country

But I have protected myself, I have watched from a safe corner
The rape of mountains, the eagle's reckless plunge.

Ever since high school I have waved goodbye to history:

I have assisted you to grow
In all ways that were convenient to me.

What is a block vote against steam shovels?

My current events teacher was a fine man
But his moral precepts were a put-up job and I followed them.

Well-dressed, in my new Adidas
At every gathering I investigated my psyche with friends

And they investigated theirs with me.

But whenever Trouble came in the front door I ran out the back
And fell into the pit of my bones.

Escaped from those burning buildings, the past,
What balance can any of us hope for?

I was comparing lipsticks
The day Nagasaki vanished.

The day Solzhenitsyn disappeared into the Gulag
I was attending a cocktail party.

Perhaps there are only ashes in my handbag.

A man at the corner of Broadway and Forty-Second Street
Tried to sweep me into a trash barrel and I almost agreed.

Already the dried blood was sifting along my wrists.

Already my own hands
Were tightening around my throat

But Sorrow saved me, Sorrow gave me an image
Of bombs like human tears watering the world's gardens.

How could I not answer?

Since then I have been planting words
In every windowbox, poking them to grow up.

What's God, that he should be mindful of me?

Sometimes I feel like wood
Waiting for someone to peel me.

Indeed I have been lukewarm
At heart, which is all that matters.

But I am afraid of disappearing
Into the wheat fields of a future

Of tiny bread-colored atoms,
Equal fragments equally dispersed

That love each other and are never hungry.

What have I ever ignited
That warmed anyone?

I have not followed the rivers.

Dangerous as a pine needle
Packed in among others, in the dense multitudes

And dry timbers of the West

I am afraid of greed,
The rich taste of it, the anger

Hidden in my pockets.

Columns of smoke on the horizon,
Pillars of green fire.

But I have arrived here somehow,
Neither have I stopped talking.

Numberless are the kitchens I have sat in,
Chewing my fingers, trying to say something,

Anything, so that the daughters of men should see
As many sides of themselves as possible.

Word after word my footprints
Have stumbled across deserts.

How should I escape them?
They keep following after me.

A little wind stirs itself,
Whisks across my eyelids,

And I know what it is before I say it:

What if the world really articulates itself
In the socket of a human knee?

God save me
From the swamps of hubris but it may be, it may be.

Before the idea, the impulse.

I feel it moving in me, it is there
Arthritic but still powerful, a seizure

Delicate as grasshoppers, a light
Gathering in the skull.

Between thumb and forefinger
And the ballbearing joints of the tongue

In soft, glottal convulsions
Out of no alien skies

But out of the mind's muscle
The hieroglyph figures rise.

The little histories of words
Cannot be eaten.

I know it, you know it
And the children...

But the images we make are our own.

In the cool caves of the intellect
The twisted roots of them lead us

Backwards and then forwards.

If only we could understand
What's in our pockets is for everyone!

I have a dictionary in one hand, a mirror.

Strangers look at themselves in it,
Tracing the expressions they use

From one family to the next
They comfort themselves, murmuring

The tongues we speak are a blizzard
Of words like warm wool flying:

In the shy conjugal rites
Of verb, consonant, vowel,

In the dark mucosal flesh lining
The prismed underside of the skin

Each one is a spark sheared
From the veined fleece of the spirit

Of the looking-glass body we live in.

It is the one I have been cherishing,
The one all of us speak from,

For the world as we know it moves
Necessarily, by steps.

Breath, pulse beat, ten digital stops.

At the foot of the mountains I look up. Does God
Lift up His hand to cover them?

Blinded by tears like rain
My bones turn granite, the spine of the hills congeals them.

Where is the eye of the storm,
Or where is the center of my seeing?

The wind of my breath is a hurricane:
I am locked inside myself.

Painfully, up the bald stepladder I climb,

[76]

But sometimes the light in my head goes on
More like the sun than a match.

Just as they said in Arabia

There's a huge pantalooned angel swelling
Inside the body's glass jar.

The white-haired thread of steam
From the teakettle on the range whistles

And sharpens itself into a voice

Bodiless as history, invisible
But still whispering in ears

That keep trying to hear it.

It is as if midgets were bellowing their names
Down sets of cardboard cylinders.

But we have not disappeared
Yet.

My friends, we have said many things to each other

In new combinations, seed upon seed exploding
And blossoming in kitchen gardens.

I confess I am ashamed of myself:

I have not tried hard enough to understand
Or listen to you speak.

But the Word is mindful of itself
And always has been.

Littering every street

In the sly eyes of tin cans,
Drops of water in the gutter

The world looks back at us

From every known language:
Yoruba, Hebrew, Chinese,

Arrogant English, the subject
Subjecting all to its desires,

Even the softer tongues, romantic

Self-reflexive, done to
As we would be done by,

Whatever life we cultivate
Out of the animal moans of childhood

It is all wheat fields, all grass
Growing and being grown.

With poisoned bread in my pockets, or gumdrops,
Or armies like Myrmidons rising

What I say is true
For a time only, thank God,

If I have arrived anywhere it is to look
Carefully, at all I thought I knew.

In living rivers of speech
The reflections I make are my own

And yet not:

Though the old growth rings are hidden from us
And the echoing tomorrows of the acorn,

The warm currents of the senses
Are a two-way street, my friends:

The palms of our hands are crisscrossed
With as many intersections as a leaf.

V

THE INTERIOR MUSIC

In the Lap of the Body

The mind an eggplant in high heels! Yes
    The mind falling in love with music, with Venetian Doges
And Renaissance Princes, the mind mixing matzo dough,
    The mind taking elocution lessons and knitting,
The mind rushing through libraries like a hollow tube
    That sucks up everything,
The mind dazzling itself in the glass labyrinths
    Of Bach and Mozart, the mind soaring through the grand architecture
Of the Idea of History,
    The mind imagining everything has a beginning
If not a foreseeable end,
    Except music only chaos, clusters of random acts scattered
Like stars the mind pushes through
    With the narrow beam of a laser, the mind beginning to grow
Like a hungry snowplow that keeps heaping up
    More blackness each year, the mind having solved itself
As mere accident, after the destruction of history
    The mind insisting on its own limits, the mind knows what it knows,
The mind settles for trying to solve other people,
    Wishing to ignore telephone messages
And dentists' appointments, especially sad matrons
    Cooped up in their limousines, complaint after spoiled complaint,
The mind of a proud woman like a wasp's nest
    Trapped in its own digestive system,
The mind constantly going to the hospital with its family
    In despair, endlessly talking to the doctors
And then coming home to call the babysitter, make plans
    It knows it will have to keep, the mind familiar with bus schedules
And back stairs, with commercial toilets and townhouses
    The mind managing offices, hiring and firing secretaries
As often as necessary, the mind doesn't want to get its feet wet
    But the mind keeps right on greeting people and remembering them,
The mind skillful as a ticket-taker wielding a butter knife
    With plump flashing hands, the mind wearing purple

To set off its gray hair, the mind *hates* its own efficiency,
    The mind aware of its own shadows
And running from them, the mind wearing white gloves,
    The mind wants to lose itself before Einstein
And then Palestrina, the clear distances of Vermeer,
    Like a calm blinkered cow standing in its stall
The mind wants to watch the world go by
    Without having to join it, how the mind suffers
The mind says to itself, but then takes itself to task
    Like a mother, the mind powerful as an eggbeater
Dutifully goes on Peace Marches, watches election booths
    And wipes noses, the mind can't help itself,
In the dark hive of the arteries all the bees are alive
    Every minute, bursting like a ripe tomato
And ransacking every garbage pail and conversation
    The mind races through laboratories and cathedrals,
The mind tries to control itself but it can't,
    Even when it is cucumber-cool, an adult
Concealing itself behind crisp curtains
    The mind never looks forward or back
With anything less than interest, a fat vegetable
    To be prodded thoughtfully, to see what seeds it will bear,
Though the mind wants to give up everything
    Especially as the veins harden, as all smooth surfaces wrinkle,
The mind thinks it has forgotten everything it ever knew
    Even about lovemaking but it certainly hasn't,
Lying in the lap of the body
    The mind does what it has to, the mind knows its own odors
And cold sweats, brooding into the ground
    Like a tired watermelon the mind knows it will leave nothing behind
Of any substance but the mind remembers itself like a tower
    With flights of doves beating in it, music it still hears
And will hear to the end, the absolute pitch rising
    Out of the black earth of the garden, the brown body of a violin
Or a whole orchestra humming to itself, pouring over everything like the wind.

The Moving Van

Is waiting outside, it is always waiting
Ominous, offstage, with the powerful motor running

In Chekhov it is the sound of the axe, nowadays
The computer says it is time to go, time to pack up,
On to the next act.

At the cocktail party we cling to our friends
In the jaws of evening, in the apricot sheen of the sky

Over the polished floor in a shimmer of topaz
Each separate face is distinct, dearer

And dearer than ever as the sun goes down
In halos of dust motes we are ranked

Around the room like a choir of modern angels
All singing together, with the help of the wine and the martinis

Each face is a sunflower, flushed in the afterglow
And tilted curiously, every which way

Under the cover of gossip, chitchat, the tiny fingernails of wit
Each watches the other, even the most sour

Over the winey Greek olives,
Over the salty bones of the anchovies even the most sweet,
The ingénue warbles her swan song but keeps one eye out for the others

For why else have we come here, over the toasted rounds of bread
With the children underfoot, with the old bore in the corner?

Dipping into the pâté, we keep stealing looks
At each new wrinkle, each new strand of gray hair

Even as each one of them, each sad sign of change
Slowly softens into dusk, as the final curtain hovers

Over the interminable monologues, the last-minute jokes,
Throat-clearings, fidgets, the little half-conscious sighs

We heave into the room like gloves, the invisible hooks of wrist watches
In between drinks punctuating sentences to remind us

The moving van is still there, a workman removes the last chair,
The prompter urges us to hurry but we can't do it,

Though the dust covers are waiting, in the wings
We will never return to the capital, this play will never end

If we can help it, the host thinks we will never leave
And maybe we won't, standing on one foot

And then the other, it is so hard to say goodbye
Over and over we keep telling each other the story of our lives.

The Reading Club

Is dead serious about this one, having rehearsed it for two weeks
They bring it right into the Odd Fellows Meeting Hall.
Riding the backs of the Trojan Women,
In Euripides' great wake they are swept up,

But the women of the chorus, in black stockings and kerchiefs,
Stand up bravely to it, shawled arms thrash
In a foam of hysterical voices shrieking,
Seaweed on the wet flanks of a whale,

For each town has its Cassandra who is a little crazy,
Wed to some mystery or other and therefore painfully sensitive,
Wiser than anyone but no one listens to her, these days the terror
Reaches its red claws into back ward and living room alike,

For each town has its Andromache who is too young,
With snub nose and children just out of school
Even she cannot escape it, from the bombed city she is led out
Weeping among the ambulances,

And each community has its tart, its magical false Helen
Or at least someone who looks like her, in all the makeup she can muster,
The gorgeous mask of whatever quick-witted lie will keep her alive
At least a little while longer, on the crest of the bloody wave,

That dolorous mountain of wooden ships and water
In whose memory the women bring us this huge gift horse,
This raging animal of a play no one dares to look in the eye
For fear of what's hidden there:

Small ragdoll figures toppling over and over
From every skyscraper and battlement hurtling
Men and women both, mere gristle in the teeth of fate.
Out over the sea of the audience our numb faces

[87]

Are stunned as Andromache's, locked up there on the platform
Inside Euripides' machine the women sway and struggle
One foot at a time, up the surging ladder
Of grief piled on grief, strophe on antistrophe,

In every century the same, the master tightens the screws,
Heightens the gloss of each bitter scene
And strikes every key, each word rings out
Over our terrified heads like a brass trumpet,

For this gift is an accordion, the biggest and mightiest of all,
As the glittering lacquered box heaves in and out,
Sigh upon sigh, at the topmost pitch a child
Falls through midnight in his frantically pink skin.

As the anguished queen protests, the citizens in the chorus wail
Louder and louder, the warriors depart
Without a glance backwards, these captains of the world's death
Enslaved as they are enslavers, in a rain of willess atoms

Anonymity takes over utterly: as the flaming city falls
On this bare beach, in the drab pinewood hall
The Reading Club packs up to go; scripts, coffee cups, black
stockings,
Husbands and wives pile into the waiting cars

Just as we expect, life picks up and goes on
But not art: crouched back there like a stalled stallion
Stuffed in its gorgeous music box is the one gift
That will not disappear but waits, but bides its time and waits

For the next time we open it, that magical false structure
Inside whose artifice is the lesson, buried alive,
Of the grim machinations of the beautiful that always lead us
To these eternally real lamentations, real sufferings, real cries.

Mahler In the Living Room

Low to the ground, the windows are full of lake water.
Leaden, the pure slabs rise straight up into the air

From the summerhouse, where we sit watching them,
Shivering on the threshold of late fall

As the bronze hills in their shabby coats
Arch themselves like hands over a cold radiator—

And Mahler in the living room like an earthquake. Behind the eyes
Sorrow heaves upward, the heavy planks of it gigantic

As armies at a distance, as oak trees, as the tar surface
Of a road giving way to frost, buckling under and over

To the white forces of winter; the underground tears bent
Like ribs cracking, hundreds of paralyzed veins

That are now, suddenly, released, in great silver floods
Powerful as oceans our whole lives rise up

Into a sky full of planets tumbling and shooting,
First lavender, then apricot, then plum-colored:

Hissing like skyrockets they streak
Over the slumberous oars in the depths voluptuously rowing

Velvet as elephants, whose liquid footsteps wallow
About to submerge everything: dock, landing place, lawn . . .

But there are jagged slashes too,
Impertinent brass flourishes, horns that bite air

And bray at each other like gold rifles

Over the little pebbles, the quaint Chinese sparrows
Of the piccolos humorously yammering, trying not to listen

To the huge hesitation waltz beneath them,
The passionate kettledrums rolling

In the throbbing cradle of the gut
Sighing over and over Let Go,

Abandon yourself to the pain, the wild love of it that surges,
Resistless, through everyone's secret bowels

Till the walls almost collapse, our clothes fall from us like leaves
Trembling, helplessly tossed

In an uncontrollable windstorm, the branches weave and sob
As if they would never stop, unbearable the sky,

Unbearable the weight of it, the loss, solitude, suffering,
The hills staring at us blindly,

The house nothing but a shell, the bare floors
Relentless, our eyes welling over with such pain

It is all absolutely uncontainable, in a few minutes
Surely everything will dissolve...

When the first duck of a new movement appears

In the middle distance, the bottlegreen oboe bobs
Blue-ringed, graceful, under the little rowboat;

The invisible red feet sturdily paddle
Like webbed spoons in the chill soup of the water

That turns into a flatness now,
The agonized surface lies down

In the glass eyes of the windows,
Those solid transparencies

We orchestrate ourselves
To keep the world framed, at bay

As the great lake of the symphony sways
Far down, far down

The violent sun sets,
Over the wet shingles, the shining flanks of the house

The threadbare arm of the hills sinks,
The wave of feeling rests.

Though It Is Hard / For Sons

Men cry
So seldom

It is a painful
Relief

To see them:

Though it is hard
For sons

Seeing a grown man
Broken

Wrenched like a nutcracker
Over somebody's shoulder

Lip twisted, snarling
Like a lion

Tears battering the white face

They may break down
Others with them

Or they may learn to walk
In wide nervous circles

Not touching,
Carefully

Around their own sons

Only in darkness
At theaters will they give in

One of them I know
At least once

Remembered:
Waking, I found him weeping

For the great gap that lies waiting

Another I did not see
But he told me

All the way into exile
With his twin sons

All three wept
Continuously

For many days,
Softening

Under a green rain

Helplessly they sat
Like women, some would say

This relief was enormous

The Interior Music

For each morning a tune
       surfaces quietly,
              what is it, where

almost invisible, a bee
       drifting through fringed clover

threads itself through a drowsy needle:
       in the familiar fields
          of the head

the interior music, waking
       collects itself into small fluent eddies
             piled up against the fence of morning.

As sleep slowly winds down
       the heavy grooves keep turning
          languidly on the pillow

and what symphony has been conducting itself here
       or quartet, or jazz solo

why this particular piece
          of loose ribbon dangling

no one knows for certain,
       but picking it up, smoothing it

and then recognizing it, the pulse
          jolts to a startled halt:

over the body, that vague switchboard
       talking to itself

what strange calls have been made here
in our absence?

All night long the connections
keep humming and whirring

in dense octaves,
layer upon layer in forkfuls
lean, many turreted structures

playing all by themselves
in the dark

inside everyone the music
clicks its combinations and comes out
here:

even when the plucked string
is pure jingle, ridiculous
as a dropped handkerchief

it feels like home:
murmuring into its chest
like a cello

the whole field lights up
to the tips of the fingers

or falls on its knees
in the rain

as the cobweb melody clings to us
in long filmy strips,
wisps of theme unravelled

all day it accompanies us
>
> like the two braceleted notes
>> of a phoebe

plaintive in the late afternoons
> and then evenings, as if we had been printed
>> with infinite horizons

stars imperceptibly move over the blackness
> behind closed eyes

with the blurred after-images of planets,
> tiny pinpointed spheres, glimpses

of entire systems breathing:
> cadences, chords, harmonies

in flocks of precise dots,
>> whole echelons of information soaring

behind our backs:
> over broad avenues and side streets,

out of stalled logjams, in sudden
> shining cadenzas of spray

bridge after elegant bridge flings
> its long lingering arch on air,

the sweet receding phrase
> that keeps reminding us of the fine lines,
>> the barely visible network

that supports all bridges, once we have seen it
> time after time

out of the darkness the quick flash
        of the complicated gold harpstrings
            of the mind.

FULL CIRCLE

In the Aquarium

From the front door to the back garden
The guests stream through the house in a straight line

And then stop, milling around on the windy lawn
Like dark fish in an aquarium

Restlessly, under the night sky,
The moon like a superior ship driving us

Just short of the small, protectively calm pool
We have formed around our blind friend

Who is backed up against the wall in a thick sweater
Clumsily buttoned over one breast.

While cold fingers the naked arms
Of the rest of us, shifting our feet

Like blinkered horses at the curb, we nod
And concentrate on each other uneasily,

From time to time twitching our skins
Under the trees waving like seaweed

Under the open eye of a moon
Our blind friend cannot see but must feel—

Cloudy illuminations like a hand stirring the water,
Our jewelled scales, our neat tails shifting

In and out of the shadows swimming
Below the second-floor windows, in the lamplight,

Where, suddenly, I notice,
Like a fist looming against glass,

The sinister bulk shape of someone watching us
So secretly I begin to shiver;

Under that arrogant gaze
Guiltily I go on watching our blind friend

And being watched myself,
Like drowned sailors we are all of us unaware

Of anything more than a few of the undercurrents
Drifting through the bowl of evening;

So many alien stars, red coral reefs growing
From the glass floor of the garden,

Drinks flashing, one or two watchdogs, cats
With their strange fixed stare.

Young Men You Are So Beautiful Up There

Young men on the roof watching the stars,
Young men your silhouettes are like tall bears
Standing against the night sky.

Young men leaning on the railing / eagerly
Watching the fire balloons you have sent up sail away

Into the heavens like burning pumpkins,
Eagles bearing messages in golden bottles,

Young men you are so beautiful up there
What if one of your fire balloons

Should pass through the open belfry of a church
And sail on, into the desert beyond?

Instead of blazing / in a bush
What if you should incinerate a small hut
A farmhouse, maybe even the whole world. . .

What if one of your fire balloons should land
On the heart of the wife who is sleeping below you

Dreaming of you, turning and turning
So that she rises up

Like paper, all aflame
Passionately shaking herself into ashes. . .

Young men you are so beautiful up there
Surely you must understand
Nobody can stop them, the fire balloons

Once they have sailed away
They will keep on going and going

Over the heads of a few farmers watching for satellites,
Over the body of your dead mother

Who is sleeping below you,
Who is breathing the heaviness of lead,

Who is waiting and waiting for you to come down
Out of the heavens into her arms.

3 Sisters 3

That woman I jumped out of
In such a hurry, a sprout

Full of juices and squawks yelling
For her to water me at once,

That woman, my own
Wet beautiful mother's long gone now,

Leaving me with nobody but these two
Dry step sisters, crones

With kneecaps for faces, coathangers,
Sterile needles to the sky,

Strange totem poles with their backs turned,
Grinning at me with their necks,

With the red Exit signs of their lips flashing
Crazily, on and off,

These last of the three sisters,
Spindly smoke signals of our lives

Tall as legbones they hang
Over the cold ashes of the fire

I sit by, chewing stale bread
And leathery raisins, disgusted

But also afraid of them,
I am no relative of these, I cry

Where is my yeasty mother
For warmth, for smoothness, for butter

Why has she left me with these black

Stones in the pudding, sticks
Of leftover straw in the oven?

Between my sheets they flank me,

One of them measuring me, a mirror
Upside down beneath a photographer's hood,

The other snapping the scissors of her thighs
Angrily, back and forth.

Bald-pated, glowering and drooling
They are sucking the life from my lungs

But they are the only issue
That is left to any of us, at the end,

Though the picture has yet to be developed
Even my midwife mother would insist

There is nothing to do but lie here
In a bed covered with black flies

With an arm around each of them,
My own two

Babies with bad eyes.

Back at the River: For Nicholas

Envoi:

O all matters of the air
As water, the warmth of fire,

All that attended his presence here
And waits upon him there,

So simple the first movement,
So subtle the tug

Finally this feather, breath
Curls up like smoke,

Gentle as a boat at evening
Drifts over the horizon.

1
The bell rings, and the voices speak
Always at dawn, always

Of ambulances in the night,
Red eyes winking by the river.

We had no time to prepare.
Possibly in our sleep

A star shot out of the sky,
An instant of bird at the window, a leaf—

Stop, thief!

If you must pick our pockets
Beware unburdening us too soon.

In the chill of this room
At least keep your fingers to yourself
Or hold your hand upon us
Heavier, heavier—
You were a sackful of gold coins
We bore lightly, on shoulders showered
By your serene radiance,
Blue-eyed, dear and gentle thief

Not so fast!

Stop spilling
All our pockets empty. Stay.
Our backs bend for you.

We can fill up again
but you, dolphin boy, our darling

Why go
Riding off on your own?
In the chill of this room
Dear, son
You have unburdened us too soon.

2
The dull thud of a baseball hits the glove.
Sharp as the crack of a bat the cry
Finally is upon us, o stop the clock
Too fast, fast—
Hush. To strike out
Is not to be alone. At first
Every time any one of us
Stammered the news on the telephone

Each house hinged itself in half.
But having for haven only
One house among us,
While the stifling darkness
Poured rain on the roof
We kept the fire up:
One red eye
Stared at the sky.

And still we keep the fire up.

Hands inevitably rise,
Feet fall, in slow motion
Here we are again,
Back at the river
Each with the same offering:
Taking whatever comfort is
Other's comforting,
In the confused, protesting crowd
Stumbling on the wet grass,
We speak of him to each other:
Breathing on such sparks
Humbly we keep his spirit
Housed against the dark.

And knowing we have forever now

The sun in his flight stopped,
Stayed, cradled in our arms,
The long glance under the lashes
Lifting across the sky,
Not to be changed, never to wither
Or lose its lovely leaves,
Out of the eye of time we snatch
The miracle he made:
The leaning tree we tended
Shelters us in its shade.

Horse
(for Pat Grean)

That day we buried your son
O wild eyed

Wild gaunt horse
Stalking down the aisle

Lean flagpole
Reaching

Face stained red
Hollow blue pupils

Bent under tough eyebrows
Like leather

Body at half-mast
Struggling
Rags flapping in air

Yes there was a horse

Grief was digging at it
Kicking at it with its heels

Into abandoned craters
Cemeteries away

We thought we would never see you again

But you came back
One day, with the sound

Of trumpets, wild
Comfortable laughter

You held our hands
In the dark

By the side of the dark sea

You took us walking
Calmly, in the park

Showing us the leaves
Turning green, rooted

Once again, explaining
Which plants to pull up

And which not, covering
Everything for winter

You did not learn to ride that horse
For nothing

Full Circle
(for Cam Grey)
1929–1979

1
Next door it has been quiet
Almost a year   since she vanished

Into the meatgrinder   cells
Monstrously exploding   gone

But still we hear her   sometimes
On the other side of the wall

The hoarse voice calls our names

As it often did, toward the end
Approaching as she disappeared

She swore she would come back,

But sitting in the weak sun
Defiant, painting her toenails red she'd relax

Only a few minutes,
Then get up and roar off

In her high powered car to telephone a lover
Or check up on a friend   or her two sons,

She said she wanted to trust us

But jaunty in her slim blue jeans,
Brief ponytail wagging

When we went out to eat together
She always paid for herself,

She'd stiffen against us, insisting
We were to be taken care of   first

But with what delicacy in her shoulders
And what humor in her wrists!

Casual as chrysanthemums
Spicy, lining fall borders

In her flaming extremities what contempt
For the white gloves of a past

She still drank, still chain-smoked bitterly
On runaway grownup feet to avoid,

For she was a lion of great power:

Because she had deserted them   once
She wrote to her parents faithfully

Crossed oceans to visit

But even in the middle of a smile
Her friends had learned, long since

To be careful of it, the sudden
Fierce show of white teeth

For she was afraid of us   also
Stupidly we did not know

Out of our own terminal ache

We kept trying to protect her,
Kept trying to turn her

Into an equal   our own
Far-off   younger sister

2
But by then it was impossible:
After the first operation

She had been given five years
At most, she told us,

She knew the enemy was coming,
She was ready

Having done her research   worrying it
As if it were raw meat

She drew up her papers   arranged
What she would leave to the children,

Angular, ginger-haired, she laughed

With tears in her eyes   laconic
As any sage in her belly

Hungrily she would read
All night on the tightrope

From one nervous cigarette to the next

But in case of the worst she collected herself,
Stored drastic caches of medicine.

In the morning we'd go for walks,

We'd talk about clothes   we agreed
On suicide as a right

For she was a lion of great power:

Asking and not asking
All the days we knew her

Passionate, excited   but still tentative
The hoarse voice called our names

With quick fingers ransacking
Religion, philosophy, science

She pored over the texts   brilliantly

Leaving whole paragraphs of illumination
On scraps of paper at our door

3
And would not stay to be thanked.

Wrapping herself in a thin quilt
To keep warm

She told no one   of course
When it began to happen

She said it was a headache
Maybe she even believed it

She said it was the bed giving her a backache
She bought three new mattresses in one week

And we thought she was mad

As the sparks smouldered, the disease
Hidden from everyone sprouted

in the dry timbers of her brain

Suddenly she was shouting
Over the smallest things she fought

Or laughed   for no reason

The words in her mouth twisted
Turned inside out,

All at once she'd subside

Into the most desperate
Curiously awkward hugs

"Sweetheart," she called everyone   staggering
On the brittle pipes of her legs

Until, finally, they took her away
To a hospital in the north

For the flames had invaded the whole house
Before she knew it:

For all her preparations,
The papers drawn up, the pills

There was no strength left to do it,

The last time we saw her
In her jersey nightgown like a teenager

Woozy   dragging on a last cigarette

Having pushed us all away
With half truths   we had to believe

Vaguely the white face waved
High in a window   behind smoke

4
And down here at the end of the telephone
All we could do was rage

At the animal howls   the thin figure

Shrunk to child-size   the convulsions
The shaved head   in the bonnet,

But now, slowly, we begin
Little by little to accept it

For she was a lion of great power:

Though time shreds her into sawdust,
Though the house next door disintegrates

Into bells clanging, into fire
In the blazing stables of her eyes,

Though we look at ourselves   lost
In the empty movie theater of the world,

In the books she left us   in the mirror

Still, on the other side of the wall
The hoarse voice calls our names

For she swore she would come back:

The worn sweaters she left us
Shyly, put their arms around us,

In death daring what life did not,

Something reminds us, wrapped
In these rough fibers

If giving and taking are one

This circle that is ended
Is only half begun.

VII

SITTING TOGETHER IN THE LAMPLIGHT

The Beautiful Building of the Present

I walk to a corner of the beautiful building of the present
Which is white, soft, and low,

Which is all lit up, which is blooming gently, which is perfumed
But inside it there is something I dislike

And a person comes up to me and leads me slowly away...

But this keeps going on all night!
I keep walking to a corner of the building of the present
Humming gaily, in all its illusory excitement

And the same person or someone just like him
Comes up to me and leads me away

Exactly the way it happens at coming out parties,
Also at church weddings, and funerals

Even though all I can see is our two heads, cut off,
Moving steadily past me on a huge silver screen

The person could easily be the principal of my school
Or my mother or my father

Or it could be the minister
Or a new boyfriend or girlfriend

But really it is my brother, my sister, it is you
My twin soul walking beside me

With absolutely no authority
We are going to try to take ourselves out of all this!

But the sequence keeps repeating itself
Like a stuck record or a trick movie film

For there is no more Malden, Massachusetts
As there is no more Hanover, New Hampshire

Neither for you nor for me, for time, naturally
Has gobbled up everyone's true birthplace

In the beautiful building of the present
Everything real and unreal

Has vanished long ago,
It disappears even as we approach it,
Floating in the thin air of a future

Which refuses to wait for us,
Which will not even *be* there
When we get there.

Lost

Miles from here, in the mountains
There is no sound but snowfall

The wind rubs itself against the trees
Under its breath,

If a crow calls it is nothing,
If a branch breaks it is nothing.

The birches look at themselves in the water,
The long white poles of their bodies waver

And bend a little,
The yellow leaves of their hair

Like pieces of far off stars come falling,
Hissing onto the lake

That is smooth as pewter, that is clear
And tranquil as an eye

Lost up here in the mountains
As if someone had dropped it, but no

The pebbles beneath the surface
Have no nerves, they are calm

If a fish leaps it is nothing
Surrounded by moss and blueberries

Flowers breathe among the rocks
So quietly you forget everything

Up here on the crusty grass
The bushes sparkle with ice

And no footprints anywhere,
If a twig snaps it is nothing

For nothing matters, once you have lost it
Down here in the valleys among the people

The sidewalks are full of holes,
Faint memories of far off lakes

Up there in the mountains,
In the great evergreen forests

If a woodchuck whirrs it is nothing,
If a bluejay shrieks it is nothing,

Pine needles slip from the trees, silently
They pile up on the ground.

Whether a Bright Stranger

And though there is no hand to push it,
No human being near,

The door heaves open, a chest
In the slow, horizontal impulse

Of household air coming in

And then going out again,
Mowing the dust of the threshold

With the barely perceptible creak
Of tiny, irritable crickets

Weeds in the cracks underfoot
Lift up their heads for a moment, the tips

Fray at the edges after each ponderous brush

And then bow down again, whispering
Under the blunt scythe of the arc,

And though there is no house around it,
No frame, no walls, no roof

The entrance and exit are real:
Memories of feet coming in

Or going out, on the worn sill
Slivers of old paint,

Faint signatures of lives
Almost finished, gone through

But still preserved, on the other side

With the soft haymows of childhood, hot tar,
Stickball on city streets...

As if the world were all window

From the non-chimney there is no smoke,
Like rays of light through the pupils

Birds plummet through the openings

And whether we are awake or asleep
Makes no difference,

Whether it is the shy embrace of a friend
Halting itself, in mid-air

Or whether it is a bright stranger

Winged, wearing a red baseball cap
Slouches against the doorjamb,

Morning and night they keep coming:
Seagulls, barn swallows swoop

From every hillside like breath
Over the non-doorstep

Sometimes even a stray dog, or a child
Or a truck, rumbling over back roads,

All that is other comes

As the secret leaves of the lungs open,
Then close, then open again, idly

Under the distant fingers of the sun.

Across the Water

The bird of music pokes holes in the air

And we listen to them, distinct
Stepping stones across the water

Where the skin of the earth is stretched tight
Often it lets go, in ripples of fine gauze

The ordinary takes off its mask

Whenever I lie down for a minute
And stop talking, and listen

As from a sickbed I see you

Swathed in unaccustomed silence
And separated from myself, it is so strange

In a gold pouring of sunlight

Each wrinkle is a green valley, each bald spot
The triumphant bare crown of a mountain,

High overhead a jet rumbles its tin lid
But all around it, in soft bubbles

Sound shapes itself as sight:

Limned in blinding light,
Layers of transparent embroidery shimmer

With the intricate running and walking stitches

Of bands practicing, football signals
Babies, screen doors slamming

Outside our windows the whole town
Expands before us like silk

As the ice cream wagon comes tinkling,
Tossing its tiny pebbles

And everything in the room stops!

Each particle is familiar, each plain face
Magnified by the threat of absence

All that we love appears

Articulate as each leaf
On the tree of the large passenger liner

That is always hovering, across the water
At the outermost edge of the harbor

Filled with the throb of orchestras,
Sad dance music, clouds of departing wings

In the present that is always leaving us
Suddenly everything becomes clear

As one or two low voices speaking
Directly, in our ears.

Sitting Together in the Lamplight

Past forty it begins.
The houses lose their heads

At dusk, in every small town
Sitting together in the lamplight

Shadows begin to take shape...

But no, it is not emptiness
Hearing the news of your death.

In layers of black wool
The moon and the stars go out,

Slowly the seeds take root,
The stomach of night bloats

In the deep waters
On the underside of town

A delicate coral city grows

And I swallow it, gradually
The rooms fill up, your face
Joins all the others

In the towers of my fingers
Battlements and turrets bloom

Pale stony flowers

In the courtyard of my ears
Everyone's death comes whispering

Till the black border of the moat
Around my body is beautiful

Invisible to the eye
But open to the still heavens

And filled up to the neck
With footsteps, flashing remarks,

Fragments of old voices, gestures
Waving like smoke in the grass.

After the First Embrace

We are separated   almost at once
    From every airport we are calling

As the wash of liquid heat
    Disperses itself   love

Thins out, cooling
    Over the whole globe,

But after the first embrace
    In Sacramento there will be one pocket,
    Here and there others,

A few cooking fires   friends
    That still remain to us   flickering
    Just over the lip of earth,

Gathered around the hearth signalling
    Greetings from nowhere
    Touchable...

As the messages come back, jittering
    Over the torn wires

Lying in bed, I listen
    To the tapes they send, spoken

Days past: the children
    Fly back and forth, believers

They grow tomatoes, bread
    Rises   in small ovens,

Thread knots itself into islands
    Clusters of people waving

For the lacework of our lives
    Is so fragile, by day

From East to West fingertips
    Ravel, reach for each other...

But talking all night like candles
    In the windows of the young

Though we gutter out by morning
    In Mexico, China, Greece,
        Each face cannot be present

Every minute   where are you
    Though the fabric rots   the pain

Holds us together   here
    In Cuba, Alaska, New Zealand

Fire shoots across the heavens
    Or falls in the water, stunned

Tongues speak, burning
    Chunks of meteorites whose absence

Is not absence   in this life waking
    In darkness   I hear your voices

We who are one body
    We who are one body.

For All the Sad Rain

O my friends why are we so weak
In winter sunlight why do our knees knock,
Why do we walk with small steps, ugly
And spindly as baby birds

Whose world do we think this is?
O my friends take it,
O my friends don't look at each other
Or anyone else before you speak.

I have had enough of scared field mice
With trembling pink ears,
I have had enough of damp
Diffident handshakes,

Do you think I haven't been stepped on by giants?
Do you think my teachers didn't stand me in a corner
For breathing, do you think my own father didn't burn me
With the wrath of a blast furnace for wanting to sit on his knee?

Indeed I have been pressed between steamrollers,
I have had both my feet cut off, and the pancreas
And the liver and the lungs of the one I love
Have been sucked out of my life and the air around me

Has turned to cereal, how will I stand up,
What opinions can I offer but I will not be silent,
There are dogs who keep their skinny tails
Permanently between their legs

But also there are sleek horses, as easily as there are curs
There are squash blossoms that flower around fountains
Like white butterflies, there is courage everywhere,
For every reluctant nail-biter

There are a hundred raised fists, for every broken broomstick
There are millions of bent grasses snapping
Back and forth at the sky, beating the blue carpet
As hard as they can, with the frail tassels of their hair

For every pair of eyes squeezed tight
Under colorless lids there are thousands of others
Wide-open, on the proud columns of their necks turning,
Observing everything like King Radar,

O my friends for all the sad rain in heaven
Filling our dinner plates you have ten fingers of honey
Which are your own, stretch them, stick them up
And then wave to me, put your arms around each other's shoulders

When we meet in a field with no fences
The horizon is yours, and the books and all the opinions
And the water which is wine and the best bed
You can possibly think of to lie in.

At the Party

When everyone comes together
Fighting, excited
Each one for all the others,

Men, women, children
Everyone
In one room

Because it is a matter of electricity
Because it is a matter of love
That room will take off into the heavens
And fly.

And whether it goes up and up like a balloon
Losing all its people here, there

Or whether it goes careening from pole to pole like a lost dove
Finally it is bound to bump into a mountain and give
One last performance:

Everyone will be standing up
With his arms around everyone else,

Ribbons of laughter will trail out
Over the tops of the trees,

Animals and skyscrapers will look up
Wondering...

For that room will be golden,
Lit up like a waffle
Throbbing above us like a comet

And always, everywhere
Someone will be waving from the window
Come on up, come on up.

Though We Live Between Jaws

For even though we live between jaws
Precarious, perched in the branches of trees,

Though we stagger from storm to storm

Though the eye at the center is an empty lighthouse
Scanning the blank waves,

Though the houses of our lives are holes
Scooped out of the air,

Still I would have us live here forever,
Breathing into each other's mouths

Like blown eggshells teetering
Like birdsnests, from side to side,

Though the houses of our lives are nothing

But soft puffballs, as permanent
As summer clouds, as secure

As the sudden sucking gulp of a swimmer
At the last gasp, in the pink

Blossom of the failing lungs,

Though all the beloved hands, eyes,
White foreheads, hair

All profiles of the moon
Like ancient sailing vessels shipwreck

In the shivering wrath of the ocean,
In the high gyroscope of the hurricane

Over the horizon who knows

Along the deserted miles of beach
What startled child's voice

Sharp as a seagull's cry may lift

Years later, at one of our gloves,
A handkerchief puffed up like a peony

In the froth at the edge of the shore floating
Till even the gold circle

Of the ring we make out of nothingness

May breathe once more, in the pocket
Of two crystals, in the bright

Brief world of the wave breaking.

El Dorado

(for Elena and Bob Fleisher)

By the side of the rented fishing boat he breaks
Up to the surface finally, out of the dark miles of the unknown

As if the godhead had been hooked at last!

And I gasp: not likely, not likely
But the water encasing him is so clear

The cold gray envelope is an eye
He's at the center of:

All 45 pounds of him surge
Like a jeweled arm, a monster club flashing

Solid as a gold bullet, royal ingot of the ocean
We paid for ourselves, the raw mystery of it roaring

Silently after us, at the end of a nylon line

> *And that should be the end of it,*
> *The rainbow turned into a side of meat,*
> *The great fish into steaks*

But even as we haul in, in, as the wet sack
Of the stunned body's flung down on the floor

The huge haunch runs with paint!

Iridescent as sunrise
Streams of lavender, rose, salmon

Diamond eggs of color swoop
Back from the tail, in strawberry rivulets

That ribbon along the sides, the heaving satin of a world
That is changing before our eyes!

Each color bleeds into the next
As in the open wound of a trail blaze

The bubbles swell, blister,
And swerve into each other,

The apricot, the pink, the fresh orange of dawn
Wash over the cold flanks

In lustrous coppery swags that slide,

That droop downwards, as the gleam fades,
Loops into matte, into dull bronze . . .

And still it goes on:

> *Though we shift uneasily in our seats*
> *On different buttocks, with new profiles*
> *And altered eyes we watch*

The green sparks of a thousand fireflies
Over the deep indigo, the gun barrel taut muscles

In the heat of daytime crackle:

Each freckled wing whisks
Over the side like rare mica

Or gathers into flares, into hot embers
Of red tongues that leap but then subside

Into brown, into steel, into thick ink
Into serge blue that is icy, almost black

Until it is finished, finally, we tell ourselves,
The dumb frozen body of this world

> *Will stop changing, stay put, give in*
> *To what we know is waiting*
> *Like fool's gold, at the end of the trail*

But even as the helmet head stiffens,
As the eyes in their gilded spectacles glaze,

Veil after veil of pale azure sweeps over the carcass
Like wisps of cloud at sunset

They jet stream high over the skin
Striped, whipping across the sky

As if meteors were messengers, keys to unlock a city
Of promises we wish we could believe in:

Though the straight lines of their passage frazzle,

Almost instantly they clot
Into tiny moons, sapphire blue

Pinpoints on a gay canvas, a circus
Of celestial eyes winking

> *Until it is I who give up*
> *Under my breath begging "Stop!"*
> *What will never stop, even as the stars go out*

At that moment the dorsal fin like a flag
Shoots up into the air and keeps right on changing,

Valiant, ridiculous, the heraldic pennon
Jaunty as a last hand waving

In the one reflex that is left
Flying

VIII

NEW POEMS

Lost in Translation

There's this one bird keeps waking us up
each morning at five o'clock with these little squirts
of pure music, coiled delicate gurgles in short
round blurts, buttery blobs of sweetness. Like the boy Mozart
playing games, over the silk heaven of our half sleep
now you see it, now you don't, skipping through the dark
tall trees of the orchestra, a slight breeze lifts up the tail

of Leonard's cotton pajamas and "1902!"
he mutters to himself, "That's what it's saying,"
then back to sleep, breath gently huffing
in waves of cool light. From the black
and whispering caves of the blue spruce standing
outside our open window the brief tune dangles
like gold earrings, tangerine sparks of small
fountaining fires I think I'll try to describe to my students

tonight, maybe. One of them will be explaining
something or other, she's charming, with her low blue
twisty ribbon of a voice, smart too, "Well really,"
she says, "if it's inexpressible it's inexpressible!"
So I tell them the story (I love to tell them stories)
of Leonard talking to the bird: why 1902, long before
either of us was born? Why not 1903, what was it,
what silvery piece of mica in a bird's beak

glittering out of the past came to say what:
pure gibberish? Utter foolishness? My student knows
the sweet talk of running water means nothing,
its double tongued fluting just puts words in our mouths,
but Leonard mutters again, this time lower, a vague
two-toned grumble more male voice than bird's
reedy trill. Our friend Murray Moulding

with Roger Tory Peterson in hand once spent weeks
spying on Swainson's Thrush, chasing after its elusive
high spiraling speech everywhere, even jogging along
the park bicycle trails sometimes he'd hear it
at the tip of the tallest tree like a windchime
jingling in the branches, "Talk to me, Baby!"
he might cry, under that intermittently ringing
single cascade of beads trying

just once to bring something back for the rest of us.
Probably he's out there right now, in wet fields with twigs
scratching at his eyes, "Who needs it?" my bright student
might say, but the bird speaks up again,
its tiny needle and thread notes stitch themselves
into our skin like the fragrance of wild
strawberries, something invisible on the air

that teases us to the window, "Nougatine? No Can Do?" It's
Leonard again, still mumbling and fussing
into his pillow, though he hasn't a clue he keeps
casting around for it, almost as if there really were
someone up there, high in the arms of the spruce
secret as wind leaving its messages
like drops of water, pebbles into a deep pool.

The Hills in Half Light

Or will we be lost forever?

In the silence of the last breath
Not taken

The blue sweep of your arm like a dancer
Clowning, in wrinkled pajamas,

Across the sky the abrupt
Brief zigzag of a jay . . .

All night the whiteness
And all day.

Once we have been lifted up
Into empty morning like ice

In the darkness of these white fields

Neither the ghost tracks of skis
Nor steel skates will wake us

Where we are looking for each other, separated

On the opposite hillside I see you
Miles away from me, a dot

Of faint color reddening, small bruised warmth
Opening its cranberry mouth and saying,

What are you saying?

*

Under a cold blanket

An immense loneliness stretches
In every direction with no fences.

A few sticks tweak the crusted snow:

Thin remnants of an army
Of lost soldiers.

I see footsteps ahead of me but whose

And where will they lead me, parallel
Or converging? Is it not possible there will be one jet trail

That will not vanish,

Two phantom ribbons unfolding
That will not feather themselves away?

*

Wrapped in our white parkas

In what shifting laminations, snowflakes
That mean nothing, transparent eyes spitting,

What glacier will we choose to lie on,
In what igloo rest

Barely breathing, in an air pocket
Just below the surface

Rustling beneath blizzards

Where is your foot, most beautiful
With blue toenails

I will be looking for it always

Wherever it is, next to me
In the darkness

Of rumpled white sheets,
Pale siftings, clouds

Sudden scarves of ourselves gusting
Loose, sandpapery as snow lifting

In what chill citadel of ice crystals
Will I find you?

After Lovemaking

A tree might lie down on the floor and be sleeping
With one of its doors open

And you might crawl over and lie down next to it
And put your head in and then your shoulders
And then your whole body

And there settle: as the last tick of wind
In the air overhead runs down
You can still feel it: nose into collarbone,
One hand thrown over
The husky burl of the other

It is like living inside a prayer drum.
Below the brown hide
In the rough oblong shadows
Heart heaves, soft as the thump of a priest's
Plump red knuckle.

In the darkness beneath your cheek,
In the echoing hollows of timepieces
And blizzards suddenly at rest,

After the first wild
Thrashing of green guitars
The curtains fold their wings,
The coffeetables turn into nests.

For you, who have just come down from some crazy
Live jazz electric storm of stars,

Inside the grandfather clock where the tiny man,
Woman, lopsided sun, moon
And dog barking at their heels come to nap

It is as simple as that: the passage back
To the secret garden is still open

Between you, in the leathery palm of a glove,
In handfuls of fragrant cedar
Next to the flat swell, the gingery fur of the chest,
Arms wrap themselves around a smooth trunk

That is still humming:
Sweeter than neon honeysuckle in June
It turns over, its wooden tongue blooms

But not forever. Even in full summer
Your head on the ribcage rises,
Falls with each breath
And you count them: how many more
May be left?

The children whisper to you like wrist watches,
Their jeweled feet unwind you

From crown to cellar hole tumbling
Past sticks, past tree houses,
Past even your great grandmother calling you
From the next to the last step.

Meanwhile you have climbed into the one body
You never want to leave.

After lovemaking you might think it was all over,
The tree fallen, with a great crashing,
But over the ridged outside skin like iron
Sap oozes, the faint sweat of tears
No one knows are there.

In the tall furniture of arms,
In clasped walnut palaces

On royal mattresses you might think you were rooted
Only in earth's bedroom, in boxes with no exit,

But up here in the dark red
Forgiving upholstery of a human being,
Down in one of your bellies a frog gurgles
And chunks, who can tell which is whose?

In the gold blurt of dwarf cellos,
In the soft rush of air down from the chin

Each puff slips into the other's the way milkweed,
Each tendril on tiptoe, sidles
Into the smallest notch on a new leaf.

After lovemaking you might think you had turned into a stiff
Polished oak statue of lovers everyone admires
Because it is so beautiful now, and dead

But it's not, even lying down here like a log
It keeps feeling around with its toes, it's a live tree
And you made it, and it breathes.

Dear Presence

Forgive me for even addressing you, forgetting
The absence I am to you.

Does the blood listen to its own cells?

Bumping and softly streaming
Like riverboats around the world

Let me remember chlorophyll, in a flood
Pouring through the bark of trees,

Let me remember teeth growing like boulders,

Half-finished buildings behind barricades
Gathering strength through the night

But let me not overwhelm you
In cities of my own image.

Thou shalt not be graven:

Neither in computer printouts
Nor the routine rattle of prayers.

Far off in the mountains there's a faint shining

Appearing and disappearing
In the white shoulders of snow.

But if all I am is not
Anywhere held, in whose arms

In the great bath of teeming emptiness

That crowds my house, in the kitchen
With eggs boiling, even in my study among the pencils,

Wherever you are, around the corner or high up,
Higher than the Himalayas

In such radiant air how may you be written?

In the ruined Times Square of the mind

Let me remember myself as nothing, a few scratches
Coming and going.

But whatever began this, somehow
As the wind tugs at the roof of the house in waves

I swear there is a mutter, a brief ruffle overhead
Of feathers, each time a bird passes by,

After the yearning warmth, the full sockets of mothers

What is the opposite of emptiness,
Is it only loss keeps us looking

Or something more, something beyond everything real,

This wild disappearing Shape
Comes prickling at my door?

As the judge looks up from his newspaper,

As the crocus leaps, as the child jumps,
As the horse canters into oblivion

Let me remember to keep listening

But stand beside me, Someone,
Let me feel your hand in the dark.

Whatever moves us makes us ready:

After the first bony stroke of the cue,
Across pool tables the quiet fingernail click

Each time the patterns rearrange themselves

Let me not be afraid:

As pulverized skyscrapers dissolve
In the blast of a second, in stop time

Let me remember the sun coming up

In absolute silence, placid
As it is indifferent

Over shredded tree trunks, over glaciers

Let me remember those blazing shadows
The ghost fossils of dinosaurs still present

In absences almost palpable, that breathe
Like mist across dim mirrors

We stand in front of, staring beyond ourselves

At empty shower caps, ferns hanging, white towels
Shoulder to shoulder like wings, like flannel pajamas

Flung to the floor but still crumpled in the shape
Of motionless rivers, whatever slept in them by night.

Mountainside Farm

The big box of the house teeters
Dangerously, on the upthrust edge of the world

And you sleep in it, how can you

Relaxed, quietly breathing
At the borders of morning like a leaf

Becalmed in a pool.

*

What is this clear membrane of silence
You wake to?

Windows, windows.

From top to bottom, with their small panes
Staring at the sky.

*

Something is about to happen
Without you!

Below, in the valley, the sun is a red fist
Lifting itself over the threshold.

In the pale, glistening
Transparency of an eggshell

First there is a rose
Triangle flickering in one corner,

Then another corner smokes
Into peach-colored fumes

But the room's four walls
Stand around like eyes

Not looking at you:

Invisible as a ghost
In the attic's gray wings

It is as if you were backstage
At earth's first opera.

*

As the light slowly seeps in

Under the door like water,
Long fingers that waver and reach out

Around the walls in a spreading
Lemony stain,

Liquid ribbons of it unfold

Into flaming raspberry cloths
Rippling over the bed

So mindlessly you think you might drown in it:
Gradually the room fills up

Brighter and brighter,
Baseboard, windowsill, ceiling

In gold waves of soft
Boiling fire.

[157]

*

On the other side of the earth
It's night time, people are dying

And trucks rushing at each other,

Rice slips through the fingers
Of beggars on street corners, whole cities

Going down into a darkness

That pulls at your skirts; your own children
Grow up into murderers

And nothing you do can stop it:

*

At center stage the hills
Are talking to each other, and the valleys.

In this gigantic quiet

As the great, silent
Trumpet of the sun rises

Over your head

If you are not responsible
For anything, it is a kind of comfort

And a sadness that will never leave you.

*

Soft as a prompter's cough
It brushes by you: peace, the deer

With lowered eyes browsing
In distant woods is not

Thinking of you, even the cars
On the highway are ignorant of you.

Who Goes There

1

Across the rough embrace of the cove
At the end of one arm, stuck up out of it like a bone

Square, glaring in the sunlight, eggwhite
The house could be the home of spies

It is so difficult to get to, only a small track winds out to it
Past the little clutter of cars dumped on the beach

Near Kennebunkport, patchy above the sea

It gives nothing; who lives there
No one knows,

Perhaps it is some part of ourselves
We've never met,

Bald as an outdoor movie screen but hopeful,

At dusk it puts on its gray raincoat
Flecked with coral

But still no one appears, in the last rays
Though its windows suddenly flare up

Like neon signboards in Connecticut
Over the smudged purple of the coastline

Ruthless as sunglasses flashing
By whose orders trained

On whose shoulders do they stand

These mirrors that reflect nothing but ourselves
And the dying sun, where is it

And who are we, what is it we keep looking for

2

Perhaps it is right here,
The telephone rings like a fire siren

That won't stop,
Frying bacon in the kitchen

Where was it we were supposed to be

At nine-thirty, I can't be there
Till ten after, the kid's spilled his cereal

And your mother's waiting,
She says we don't love her, there's no end to it,

The tight stomach winds itself
And then squeezes, pain comes in layers,

Bound muscles grind into each other
Like barbed wire in coils

Nailed to a low roof

Christ, when are we going to *do* something?
The children keep asking and asking,

In Geneva the chairman's threatening another stalemate

And the car's got to have its oil changed,
Sleepless, I have these nightmares,

In the hall mirror a jellyfish swims up to me,

There's a dead tree in the back yard

3

Or maybe it's something else
At the exact center of the house

Maybe it's kinder, more peaceful
Than we know

Between the slow drops
Of an old faucet

The floor feels its feet
Padding over smooth walnut planks

While everyone is asleep maybe it passes
A light finger over our foreheads

Just after the last visitor leaves

A glass of water left standing
On the dining room table ripples

Relaxed, easy as velvet

As if there were underground springs in the cellar,
Sounds no one can see

Merge into low gurgles, the soft chuckle of a child playing
By itself

All the rooms surround it,
The one room that is not there

Like open patios in Texas

In rivers of silk, in a trickle

Of invisible air from a roof ventilator
In the middle of summer, amazing

The faint odor of snow

4

That will not stay, if the mind refuses to grasp it

The generations speed by,

Your father fades into my father, who was he
And why? You know I can't hear you

For the roar of jets,
My ears are ringing, it's sheer nerve

We ride out on, frazzled
Right down to the wire,

The silence at the center of everything

Cannot be willed but lives

In the taut muscles of the shoulders
Whenever they remember to let go

As the lawnmower's urgent snarl
Shuts off, the sweet smell of grass rises

Not just out there but everywhere

The transparent ozone of space
Seeps in like a clear stain

Without your having to do anything

Listen! It will take you with it

5

Wherever it comes from, though it has no name
Out here on the West Coast, in the mountains

Looking down on a lone farmhouse
Paralyzed, in a dream

That is no dream

The valley is a bleak clamshell, bare, open,
The house in the middle of it like an eye

We tore out ourselves and left here
Staring at the sky.

The tall windows are black
Slit pupils against gray clapboards,

The stone chimney seems to shiver

As chainsaws whine in the distance,
Freight trains hurtle by

Smoke curls from it like a prayer vanishing,

Who lives here we do not know
Any more whether it is ourselves or strangers

Though the windows still keep watch, crisscrossed
By crows passing, the abrupt hunch of a hawk

In sparse grass small rodents scatter
From desert to schoolyard to space center

Wherever we are, in city traffic speeding,
Huddled behind blind skyscrapers,

Grandchildren of Detroit's red ore,
Of Chicago's nuclear reactors

Scraped together but still clinging
At the end of the century like barnacles

Faceless as cliffs we keep listening

For something, what is it, some knock
At the door. . . .

Patricia Goedicke was born in Boston, Massachusetts and educated at Middlebury College and Ohio University. She is the author of eight collections of poetry including *Listen, Love* (Barnwood Press, 1986), *The Wind of Our Going* (Copper Canyon Press, 1985), and *Crossing The Same River* (University of Massachusetts Press, 1980). Goedicke has received several national grants and awards, including a National Endowment For the Arts Fellowship, and her work has appeared in many national anthologies and magazines, including *The New Yorker, Poetry, The Hudson Review, Poetry Northwest, APR, The Kenyon Review, The Paris Review,* etc. Patricia Goedicke has been writer-in-residence and on staff at Institute Allende, University of Guanajuato, San Miguel de Allende, Guanajuato, Mexico, at Kalamazoo College, Sarah Lawrence College, and Hunter College, among others, and now teaches at the University of Montana, Missoula, Montana, where she lives with her husband, Leonard Wallace Robinson.